What Is the
MODEL
MINORITY
MYTH?

VIRGINIA LOH-HAGAN

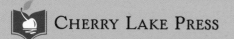

Published in the United States of America by Cherry Lake Publishing Group
Ann Arbor, Michigan
www.cherrylakepublishing.com

Reading Adviser: Beth Walker Gambro, MS, Ed., Reading Consultant, Yorkville, IL
Book Design and Cover Art: Felicia Macheske

Photo Credits: © Diego Cervo/Shutterstock.com, 5; © UV70/Shutterstock.com, 7; Library of Congress, United States. Army. Signal Corps., 1942, LOC Control No: 2003689109, 9; © 4 PM production/Shutterstock.com, 11; © DGLimages/Shutterstock.com, 12; © Asia Images Group/Shutterstock.com, 15; © mark reinstein/Shutterstock.com, 16; © F. JIMENEZ MECA/Shutterstock.com, 19; © TORWAISTUDIO/Shutterstock.com, 21; © Sang Cheng/Shutterstock.com, 22; © Christine Glade/Shutterstock.com, 25; © Iakov Filimonov/Shutterstock.com, 27; © Roman Bodnarchuk/Shutterstock.com, 29; © Logan Swenson/Shutterstock.com, 30

Graphics Throughout: © debra hughes/Shutterstock.com

Cherry Lake Press is an imprint of Cherry Lake Publishing Group.

Library of Congress Cataloging-in-Publication Data

Names: Loh-Hagan, Virginia, author.
Title: What is the model minority myth? / by Virginia Loh-Hagan.
Description: Ann Arbor, Michigan : Cherry Lake Publishing Group, [2022] | Series: Racial justice in America : Asian American Pacific Islander | Audience: Grades 4-6 | Summary: "Students will learn about the model minority myth and discover how it discriminates against and holds back Asian American Pacific Islanders (AAPI) in America. This series explores the issues specific to the AAPI community in a comprehensive, honest, and age-appropriate way. Series is written by Virginia Loh-Hagan, a prolific author, advocate, and director of the San Diego State University Asian Pacific Islander Desi American Resource Center. Developed in conjunction with educator, advocate, and author Kelisa Wing, these books were created to reach children of all races and encourage them to approach race issues with open eyes and minds. Books include 21st Century Skills and content, an activity across books, table of contents, glossary, index, author biography, sidebars, and educational matter"—Provided by publisher.
Identifiers: LCCN 2021047055 | ISBN 9781534199354 (hardcover) | ISBN 9781668900499 (paperback) | ISBN 9781668906255 (ebook) | ISBN 9781668901939 (pdf)
Subjects: LCSH: Model minority stereotype—United States—Juvenile literature. | Asian Americans—Social conditions—Juvenile literature. | Pacific Islander Americans—Social conditions—Juvenile literature. | United States—Race relations—Juvenile literature. | United States—Ethnic relations—Juvenile literature.
Classification: LCC E184.A75 L635 2022 | DDC 305.800973—dc23/eng/20211014
LC record available at https://lccn.loc.gov/2021047055

Cherry Lake Publishing Group would like to acknowledge the work of the Partnership for 21st Century Learning, a Network of Battelle for Kids. Please visit *http://www.battelleforkids.org/networks/p21* for more information.

Printed in the United States of America

Dr. Virginia Loh-Hagan is an author, former K-8 teacher, curriculum designer, and university professor. She's currently the director of the Asian Pacific Islander Desi American (APIDA) Center at San Diego State University. She identifies as Chinese American and is committed to amplifying APIDA communities. She lives in San Diego with her one very tall husband and two very naughty dogs.

CHAPTER 1

What Is the Model Minority Myth?

Asian Americans are a strong community. But like other people of color, they are suffering. They are denied justice. They struggle under White supremacy.

In the 1960s, activists first used the term "Asian American." They sought to unite Asian groups. Before this, Asian immigrants were known by their ethnicities. For example, they were called "Chinese American" or "Indian American." They acted as separate groups. But they were mistreated as one big group. So they joined forces. As "Asian Americans," they had more power.

Today, they are also called "Asian American Pacific Islander (AAPI)." Another term is "Asian Pacific Islander Desi American (APIDA)." These terms are more inclusive, meaning that they apply to more Asian people. But they don't fully represent this community. Asian Americans are diverse. They have unique cultures, histories, and languages. It's important to remember this.

Asian Americans are part of the American story. They have made significant contributions. And they continue to do so. Yet, they are often pushed to the margins. In the 1800s, they immigrated in large numbers. Since then, they have faced discrimination. They have fought to be seen and heard. Their fight for racial justice continues today.

Think about what you have learned in school. How many Asian Americans did you study?

Asian Americans have been called the "model minority." They are viewed as being very successful. They are seen as having high levels of education. They are seen as having a lot of money. They are seen as hard workers. White America sets them up to be a model. Asian Americans are used as an example for other minority groups. If they can succeed, why can't other people of color do the same? Being a "model" may sound good. But it is not. This type of thinking is racist.

The "model minority" label is based on stereotypes. It assumes several things, including that Asian Americans are smarter than other groups, they are better at math and science, they are quiet and obedient, and that they achieve without help.

Anything based on stereotypes is problematic. Being a model minority has many issues. It is harmful to the Asian American community. It is also harmful to other communities of color. It is untrue and incomplete. That's why it's called the Model Minority Myth. The stereotypes do not apply to all Asian Americans.

This book unpacks the Model Minority Myth. Learn more so that you can do more. Help fight against White supremacy.

> Think about stereotypes you have about Asian Americans. Why are stereotypes bad?

AMPLIFY AN ACTIVIST!

Activists change our world for the better. Cindy Trinh is a Vietnamese American. In 2015, she created a photo series. She called it, "The Model Minority Reality." She took pictures of Asian Americans working in low-paying jobs. She showed how many Asian Americans don't fit the "model minority" stereotypes.

CHAPTER 2

What Is the History of the Model Minority Myth?

The model minority was first coined by William Petersen. Petersen was a sociologist. He studied people. In 1966, he wrote an article in *The New York Times Magazine*. The article was titled "Success Story: Japanese American Style." Petersen celebrated Japanese American family structures. He praised their work ethic and their focus on education. He said Japanese American families had "model" behaviors. He said these behaviors helped them overcome discrimination. Petersen's article may sound good. But it caused more harm than good.

Let's put this in context. In 1941, Japan attacked Pearl Harbor in Hawaii. This caused the United States to enter World War II (1939–1945). As a result, Japanese Americans were assumed to be spies for Japan. President Franklin D. Roosevelt wanted to protect national security. He passed a law forcing Japanese Americans into camps. These camps were like jail. More than 120,000 Japanese Americans were kicked out of their homes. They were held in these camps for years. Their civil rights were taken away. After that, many Japanese Americans were fearful. They did not want to be imprisoned again. So they led quiet, lawful lives. They wanted to be accepted. They wanted to be "good Americans." They did not want to be seen as threats.

Think about how Japanese Americans were incarcerated. How is this a violation of civil rights?

Before Petersen's article, several articles were published about Toy Len Goon. In 1952, Goon was named American Mother of the Year. She was the first Asian American to win that honor. She was praised for successfully running a laundry business. She was also praised for raising eight successful children. Most of them finished college. She was an early example of a model minority. The success of Asian Americans was a trendy topic. Many newspapers and magazines wrote about their success. For example, in 1987, *Time* magazine's cover story was "Those Asian American Whiz Kids." Such stories made the myth more popular.

Two events in the 1960s further promoted the Model Minority Myth. First, there was a new immigration law in 1965. Earlier laws banned many immigrants from Asia. The 1965 law reversed these bans. It allowed more immigrants to enter the United States. It also didn't restrict immigration from Asia and other countries. But it did limit immigration to those with professional or scientific backgrounds. So Asians immigrating during this time mostly came from Far East Asia and India. They were educated. They worked in professional jobs. They made money. They bought homes. They achieved the "American Dream" faster than other immigrants.

Think about what the "American Dream" means. Does everyone have an equal chance to achieve this dream?

LEARN FROM OUR PAST!

Let's not repeat the mistakes of our past. During Japanese incarceration, Chinese Americans wanted to avoid being targeted. They wore "I am Chinese" badges. Earlier, there were immigration bans against Chinese people. Japanese immigrants benefited. They immigrated in large numbers. These groups allowed White supremacy to pit them against each other.

Think about when you worked in a group. What are the benefits of collaboration over competition?

Their success stories supported the Model Minority Myth. This myth focuses on race. Being Asian was seen as the reason for their success. But this wasn't true. These Asian immigrants had education and money. Having resources means easier access to success. The myth does not consider these contexts.

The second historical event was the civil rights movement of the 1950s and 1960s. Black Americans marched and protested. They wanted equality and freedom. They wanted to end racist policies and laws. These unfair laws benefited White Americans. They were unfair to people of color.

The Model Minority Myth was used as a racial wedge. This meant that it pitted Asian Americans against Black Americans. It allowed White supremacy to blame Black communities instead of racist laws. It let them say, "The system works. It's not the problem. See how well Asian Americans are doing. Why can't you be more like them? The problem must be you." Some activists think the Model Minority Myth isn't really about Asian Americans. They think it is more about Black Americans. They say it is not about Asian American success. Instead, it's a way to show how Black Americans are lacking.

CHAPTER 3

What Does the Model Minority Myth Look Like Today?

The Model Minority Myth still exists today. It shows up in various ways. "Tiger parenting" is an example. It is based on the Model Minority Myth. It builds on how Toy Len Goon was credited for her children's success. Some Asian American parents believe their successes are their children's successes. Success is defined by education and money.

Amy Chua is a Yale Law School professor. She coined the term "tiger mother." In 2011, she wrote a book about it. She shared her own experience as a tiger parent. Tiger parents are strict and controlling. They instill strong work habits. They expect excellence. They push their children to achieve high levels of performance. Consider Indian Americans. Indian Americans have dominated spelling bees. They have coaches and host practices. They spend a lot of time and effort on winning.

Tiger parenting is grounded in filial piety. Filial piety is a Chinese concept. It means having respect for elders. It centers the family over the individual. Children are expected to bring pride to the family. They are to be models, or credits to their family. They should also be credits to the Asian race.

Think about the term "a credit to one's race." How does this apply to the Model Minority Myth?

Think about leaders you know. How many are Asian American?

STAY ACTIVE ON SOCIAL!

Stay connected on social media. It is a great way to learn more. Follow these hashtags:

- **#NotYourModelMinority** This hashtag challenges White supremacy. It supports Black Lives Matter.

- **#ReModelMinority** This hashtag was launched by the Smithsonian Asian Pacific American Center. It shares the harmful effects of the Model Minority Myth.

Some Asian American youth do more than go to school. They engage in different activities. Their days are busy. They take music lessons and are tutored. They participate in sports. Tiger parents encourage this. They think these activities will help their children get into good colleges. Good colleges often mean good jobs.

What does a "good" job mean? Good jobs have high status. They offer high salaries. They require years of training. Many Asian Americans are pushed into STEM jobs. STEM means Science, Math, Engineering, and Technology. This is another way the Model Minority Myth shows up today. Many Asians with Far East Asian and Indian backgrounds become doctors or engineers. But these are not the only job options. There are all types of jobs. There are also different ways to be successful.

Some Asian Americans are raised to value hard work over speaking up. Asian Americans are seen as quiet. This conflicts with Western values. Being quiet isn't always viewed as a strength in the United States. As such, Asian Americans are seen as hard workers but not as leaders. They are not promoted to better jobs as much as other groups. This is yet another way the Model Minority Myth presents itself.

There is much criticism of tiger parenting and of the Model Minority Myth. Today, the myth is being rejected. Asian American activists and youth are leading this movement. They recognize the harmful effects. They feel pressured. They fear not being able to meet high expectations. They fear failing and suffer from feelings of shame. Some may feel trapped by the myth. Some may feel trapped by their parents. Jimmy O. Yang is an actor and comedian. He said, "It's never easy to disappoint your parents and pursue your dreams, especially coming from an Asian family. But I figured it was better to disappoint my parents for a couple of years than to disappoint myself for the rest of my life."

Anti-Asian hate increased in 2020. There was an increase of attacks and hate crimes. The Model Minority Myth caused some Asian Americans to doubt their oppression. It gives the idea that Asian Americans are doing well and their issues are not real. Asian Americans may deny or downplay racism. They may think their suffering isn't as bad as other groups. They have a harder time proving racism exists. The myth continues to affect people today. There is a need to dismantle it, or break it apart.

Think about the pressures you face. How can you reduce these pressures?

CHAPTER 4

Why Is the Model Minority Myth Problematic?

The Model Minority Myth is problematic for many reasons. First, it makes all Asian Americans seem the same. It suggests all Asian Americans are successful. This is far from true. Southeast Asians and Pacific Islanders struggle. Many Southeast Asians came to the United States as refugees. They escaped wars and poverty. They often immigrated with nothing. They didn't have the same resources as the Asians who immigrated under the 1965 law. Pacific Islanders suffer from being colonized. They were stripped of their lands. Their ways of living were forever changed. The Model Minority Myth ignores these groups and their issues. It glorifies the success of the few. This means many people are denied the support they need.

This leads to the second problem. Because of the Model Minority Myth, Asian American students in school are often invisible. Teachers assume they will do well. Asian Americans' special needs are denied. Their mental health is ignored. They are more likely to self-harm than other groups. They are also less likely to seek help. This is proof enough to reject the Model Minority Myth.

Think about how many countries are in Asia and the Pacific Islands. Which countries would you like to learn more about?

Think about both race and resistance. How have Asian Americans been discriminated against? How have they resisted?

Third, the Model Minority Myth only celebrates success. This causes issues. It allows White supremacy to define success. This means Asian Americans are valued only if they are "good Americans." The myth ignores the dark side of Asian American history. It does not focus on the racism and struggles. The United States is painted as a welcoming place. This is not true. Many laws and policies discriminated against Asian Americans. Asian Americans have been excluded, imprisoned, and killed. It's important to know this. Being ignorant keeps White supremacy in power. Like other people of color, Asian Americans aren't truly free. They have had to fight for their rights and freedoms. They have to keep fighting.

Fourth, the Model Minority Myth is not real. It's based on colorism. Rights are given to groups that are closer to Whiteness. But, during times of crises, these rights are taken away. For example, think about the Japanese Americans. During war time, they were incarcerated. During peace time, they were praised as the model minority. White supremacy uses the Model Minority Myth to suit its needs.

The biggest problem is how the Model Minority Myth harms the struggle for racial justice. By now, you know not to be fooled. This myth is a bad thing. Having a "model minority" means there is a "problem minority." The Model Minority Myth doesn't honor Asian Americans. It dishonors them. It uses them to diminish other groups. In this way, it dishonors all communities of color.

Asian Americans' success is used as proof that racism does not exist. The Model Minority Myth blames communities of color for injustice. It doesn't allow space to question racist policies. It places Asian Americans as partners for White supremacy. As such, Asian Americans are not seen as partners against racism. This causes tensions between Asian Americans and other groups.

The Model Minority Myth makes people of color compete with one another. It is a tool used to keep communities of color from joining forces. Communities of color are too busy fighting each other. This makes them too tired to fight against racism. Racism wins in the end.

Think about how Asian Americans have worked with other groups. Why is solidarity important?

BE IN THE KNOW!

Other concepts to know:

- **Honorary Whites** This is racist. It refers to Asian Americans having light skin tones. Whiteness is seen as the "model" or desired trait.

- **Imposter Syndrome** Model minority stereotypes are hard to live up to. Some Asian Americans may doubt themselves. They worry they're not good enough.

CHAPTER 5

How Can We Be Better?

Now you have learned about the problems with the Model Minority Myth. Let's work to abolish it. Let's stop it forever.

We all come from different positions of privilege. We also have different types of privilege. Privilege is a special right or advantage. It is given to a chosen person or group. It is not earned. In the United States, being White is a privilege. Other examples include being male or an English speaker. It's hard to get ahead in a world that is not made for you. Use your privileges. Help oppressed people achieve equality.

Start with Yourself!

Everybody can do something. Just start somewhere. Start small. Build your self-awareness and your knowledge.

- Learn more about different Asian American groups. Don't clump all Asian people together. Know the differences.

- Unlearn how success has been defined by others. Reject the Model Minority Myth's narrow definitions. Define success on your own terms.

- Learn more about Asian American history. The Model Minority Myth focuses on success stories. It doesn't focus on stories of struggle. Learn about the good, the bad, and the ugly.

Think about your privileges. What powers and resources do you have?

Be an Ally!

Being an ally is the first step in racial justice work. Allies recognize their privilege. They use it in solidarity with others. They see something and they say something.

- Speak up when you hear others supporting the Model Minority Myth. For example, stand up against this comment: "You're an Asian American. You must be great at math." You can say, "That's a stereotype. It's not true for all Asian Americans. Let's ask instead of assume."

- Speak against having to be a "model." Nobody is perfect. Become comfortable asking for help and making mistakes. Share how you need help to succeed. Share how you have made mistakes.

Be an Accomplice!

Being an **accomplice** goes beyond allyship. Accomplices use their privilege. They challenge supremacy. They are willing to be uncomfortable. They stand up for equal rights.

- Stand with Asian Americans to increase representation. For example, find out how many Asian American teachers work at your school. Talk to the principal and the school board. Encourage them to hire more Asian American teachers.

- Stand united against invisibility. Ask your teachers to include Asian American history. Make a list of books for others to read.

Think about your powers and resources. How would your life be different without them?

Be an Activist!

Activists actively fight for political or social change. They give up their own privileges. They work together to fight against racism. They understand that if one group suffers, all groups suffer.

- Fight anti-Blackness. Support Black Lives Matter. Don't allow Asian Americans to be used as a tool against Black communities.

- Fight for Asian Americans to have more voice. For example, if you get selected for a team or club, give up your spot. Suggest that an Asian American take the position instead.

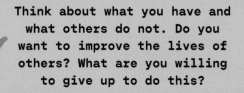

Think about what you have and what others do not. Do you want to improve the lives of others? What are you willing to give up to do this?

Take the Challenge!

Read all the books in the "Racial Justice in America" series. Engage in the community of activism. Create a podcast, newsletter, video, or social media campaign. Show up for the Asian American community. Include a segment about the Model Minority Myth.

TASK: Research events in history in which one group has been privileged over others. Show how people in power have exploited communities of color. Show the dangers of such actions.

Share your learning. Encourage others to learn more. Then, when you know more, do more. Commit to racial justice!

WHAT WOULD YOU DO?

Imagine an Asian American kid moves in next door. Your friend says, "I bet he's a crazy rich Asian. His parents must be doctors." How does this promote the Model Minority Myth? What would you do?

☐ Laugh to fit in.

☐ Ignore it.

☐ Change the subject.

☐ Say something.

EXTEND YOUR LEARNING

FICTION

Chao, Gloria. *American Panda*. New York, NY: Simon Pulse, 2019.

Jung, Mike. *Unidentified Suburban Object*. New York, NY: Scholastic Press, 2016.

NONFICTION

Loh-Hagan, Virginia. *A is for Asian American: An Asian Pacific Islander Desi American Alphabet Book*. Ann Arbor, MI: Sleeping Bear Press, 2022.

Public Broadcasting Service: Asian Americans
www.pbs.org/weta/asian-americans/

Tedx Talks.: Asian Doesn't Start with A+.
www.youtube.com/watch?v=G1Ke6JIZyX4

GLOSSARY

abolish (uh-BAH-lish) to permanently stop or end something

accomplice (uh-KAHM-pluhss) a person who uses their privilege to fight against supremacy

ally (AH-Iye) a person who is aware of their privilege and supports oppressed communities

colonized (KAH-luh-nyzd) to be conquered or to have a force take control of one's land and culture

colorism (KUH-luh-rih-zuhm) a system that discriminates against people with a dark skin tone

Desi (DEH-see) a word that describes people from India, Pakistan, or Bangladesh

discrimination (dih-skrih-muh-NAY-shuhn) the unjust or unfair treatment of different categories of people

dismantle (dihs-MAN-tuhl) to break apart into pieces

ethnicities (eth-NIH-suh-teez) the states of belonging to a social group that has a common national or cultural tradition

filial piety (FIH-lee-uhl PYE-uh-tee) duty of respect, obedience, and care for parents and elderly family members

inclusive (ihn-KLOO-siv) allowing all kinds of people to belong

myth (MITH) a story that is not true but is widely believed

privilege (PRIV-lij) an unearned right or advantage given to a chosen person or group

racial wedge (RAY-shuhl WEJ) a group used to split apart communities of color in an attempt to decrease the strength of a group

refugees (reh-fyoo-JEEZ) people who have been forced to leave their country in order to escape war, persecution, or natural disaster

sociologist (soh-see-AH-luh-jist) a scientist who studies people or human societies

stereotypes (STEHR-ee-uh-typss) widely held ideas or beliefs many people have about a thing or group, which may be untrue or only partly true

supremacy (suh-PREH-muh-see) the idea that one group is superior to other groups and thus is given privileges to maintain that power

INDEX